Thirty
sparkling gems

Peter Currie

Day One

Endorsement

Whether we have only just begun in the Christian faith or have been walking with the Lord Jesus for years, to think upon the promises of God is essential. As we journey through this life we will be buffeted by the world, the flesh and the devil. There are times when we cry out for protection, provision, guidance, strengthening, and to know that our Heavenly Father has us secure in His grip of grace.

In Thirty Sparkling Gems, *Peter Currie has collected together some of the precious promises of God which the Christian should take seriously to heart, as they will provide help, strength, assurance and much joy as we remember all that the Lord has done for His children—from those first promises of forgiveness to the certainty of the Lord Jesus Christ's return.*

These promises have been a real joy and blessing to Peter over the years, and it is his desire that others would reflect upon them so that they may make progress in their Christian lives.

Each meditation is short enough to read while on the bus or train or sitting with your morning cup of tea, yet deep enough to give you something to think about throughout the day.

Stuart Davis, Senior Pastor, Trinity Road Chapel, London

© Day One Publications 2020
First Edition 2020

Unless otherwise indicated, Scripture quotations are from the New King
James Version (NKJV)®. Copyright © 1982 by Thomas Nelson, Inc.
Used by permission. All rights reserved.

British Library Cataloguing in Publication Data available

ISBN 978-1-84625-673-8

Published by Day One Publications
Ryelands Road, Leominster, HR6 8NZ

☎ 01568 613 740
FAX: 01568 611 473
email—sales@dayone.co.uk
web site—www.dayone.co.uk

Cover designed by Kathryn Chedgzoy and printed by 4Edge

To Dr M. R. De Haan
and Dr Harry Ironside,
who taught me to trust in
the promises of God

Contents

Introduction 9

1 *The gospel promise* 12

2 *The graciousness of the promise* 16

3 *The certainty of the promise* 20

4 *The promise of friendship* 24

5 *The promise for deep waters* 28

6 *The promise of a heavenly home* 32

7 *The promise that others in our family will be saved* 36

8 *The promise of daily cleansing* 40

9 *The promise of eternal security* 44

10 *The promise of strength when needed* 48

11 *The promise of guidance* 52

12 *The promise of provision* 56

13 *The promise of a resurrection body* 60

14 *The promise of the Second Coming* 64

15 *The promise of an elect company and a warm welcome* 68

16 *The promise of a willing Guest* 72

THE BEATITUDES 76

17 *The promise to the poor in spirit* 78

18 *The promise to those who mourn* 82

19 *The promise to the meek* 86

20 *The promise to those who hunger and thirst for righteousness* 90

21 *The promise to the merciful* 94

22 *The promise to the pure in heart* 98

23 *The promise to the peacemakers* 102

24 *The promises to those who are persecuted for righteousness' sake* 106

THE PATMOS PROMISES 110

25 *The promises attached to the last book of the Bible* 112

26 *The promise to the Christian dead* 116

27 *The promise to the well clad* 120

28 *The promise to the wedding guests* 124

29 *The promise that we shall reign with Christ a thousand years* 130

30 *The promise to the washed* 134

Endnotes 138

Introduction

The Bible is full of promises. There are promises made by one man to another, promises made by man to God, and even the devil has made promises which are recorded in the Bible. However, the Bible's main emphasis is on the hundreds of promises made by God to man, and this is the focus of this book.

The promises of God recorded in the Bible are not only numerous; each one is important in its own right and of great worth—'exceedingly great and precious', as the apostle Peter puts it (2 Peter 1:4). The Bible is like a treasure chest and each promise is like a sparkling gem contained therein. They may seem insubstantial, just words on paper, but so is the money we use every day. However, in the United Kingdom, all paper money includes the words 'I promise to pay the bearer on demand the sum of . . . ' This used to mean that paper money could be exchanged for an equivalent amount of gold. This is no longer the case, but it still means that our paper money is backed by the British government and whatever wealth it possesses. This is relatively good security, but it is nothing compared to the promises of God which are backed by Almighty God Himself and 'His riches in glory by Christ Jesus' (Phil. 4:19).

The promises of God are of such great worth because they *are* the promises of *God*. We can be sure of this because they are recorded in the Bible which is the Word of God. When men wrote it down, they were not expressing their own ideas, but 'they were moved by the Holy Spirit' to write what they wrote (2 Peter 1:20–21), and the very words they used were 'words . . . which the Holy Spirit teaches' (1 Cor. 2:13).

This book contains meditations on some of the great promises of God which have meant a lot to me. I hope you, the reader, will appreciate their worth as well. The first sixteen include important subjects such as salvation, friendship with God, going through difficult times, heaven, others being saved in our family, daily cleansing, eternal security, strength when needed, guidance, provision, the resurrection body and the Second Coming. These are followed by eight meditations upon the Beatitudes, the well-known sayings of Jesus at the beginning of the Sermon on the Mount. Finally, this book considers the Patmos promises—six meditations on the beatitudes contained in the book of Revelation.

The gospel
promise

For God so loved the world that He gave His only begotten Son, that whoever believes in Him should not perish but have everlasting life.

(John 3:16)

John 3:16 is a wonderful single-verse summary of the Christian message—the most wonderful verse in the whole Bible, in my opinion. The great Protestant Reformer Martin Luther loved it and so do I—especially because it was instrumental in my conversion when I understood that 'whoever' meant 'me'.

My mother took me to church when I was a small boy. However, by the time I was thirteen my interest in Christian things had waned and in my heart I was beginning to say that there was no God, until, somehow, I was persuaded to attend the closing meeting of the Billy Graham 1966 London crusade at Wembley stadium. I do not remember much of what Dr Graham said, but I do remember that becoming a Christian was suddenly the most important thing in the world. However, I was shy and I did not respond to the invitation to 'go forward'. Instead, I went home feeling depressed, until I remembered that someone had given me a New Testament with an explanation of the way of salvation at the back. I read this right through and then came to a page entitled 'My Decision', which included John 3:16, but with the 'whoever' replaced by a blank where I could enter my name, to show that I was putting my trust in the Lord Jesus Christ as my Saviour (the second half of John 3:16 could be translated 'whoever *trusts* in Him should not perish but have everlasting life'). I remember saying to myself, 'Well, I do believe!' and being filled with joy. I feel myself to be a sinner, but that simple decision to put my trust in the Lord Jesus Christ was the beginning of a spiritual new life which has made a wonderful difference over the many years since then.

John 3:16 begins with God the Father. It is true that the Lord Jesus Christ came willingly into the world to save sinners, but it was God the Father who sent Him. The reason was His great love, so great that He gave His only Son, His beloved Son, to be our Saviour. The Lord Jesus became Man and went to the Cross for us people and for our salvation. Go to the Cross and behold the Son of God dying in agony and blood—then you will begin to understand what it meant for God to give His Son.

Finally, notice that God loved *the world*, the whole wide world. He hates our sin, but He loves the sinner. He 'desires all men to be saved and to come to the knowledge of the truth' (1 Tim. 2:4). He is 'not willing that any should perish but that all should come to repentance' (2 Peter 3:9). There is no need for anyone to 'perish' or 'be lost'. Whoever you are, whatever wrong you have done, you can be saved, if only you will come to the Lord Jesus Christ and put your trust in Him. *This is the promise of God, the gospel promise, that whoever trusts in His Son should not perish but have everlasting life.*

The gospel promise

The graciousness
of the promise

For by grace you have been saved through faith, and that not of yourselves; it is the gift of God, not of works, lest anyone should boast.

(Eph. 2:8–9)

These words were written by the apostle Paul to the Christians at Ephesus. They refer to the gospel promise, the promise of salvation, and Paul is saying that, in the case of the Ephesians, the promise has been fulfilled—note the past tense, 'you have been saved'. Also, Paul emphasizes the graciousness of the promise by saying, 'For *by grace* you have been saved through faith.'

Grace is the free, unmerited favour of God. It means that God gives us salvation as a free gift even though we have not done anything to deserve it. We are saved by grace through faith. Faith is the empty hand that takes the free gift. We are saved simply and solely through trusting in the Lord Jesus Christ. Salvation is 'not of works, lest anyone should boast'. If people got to heaven because they had done this or that, they would have something to boast about, but God will not tolerate such boasting (see Rom. 4:2). When we get to heaven, we will sing words like these:

> Unto Him who hath loved us
> And washed us from sin,
> Unto Him be the glory for ever! Amen.
> (Arthur T. Pierson, 'With Harps and with Vials')

Some Bible commentators say that the words 'and that not

of yourselves; it is the gift of God' refer to saving faith, and it is true that we cannot come to the Lord Jesus Christ and put our trust in Him without God's help—by nature sinners run away from God (see John 3:20). However, the words that follow, 'not of works, lest anyone should boast', undoubtedly refer to salvation and it seems more straightforward to say that salvation is the focus of the whole verse. Certainly, although God gives us many gifts (see James 1:17), *the* 'gift of God' is salvation and everlasting life in His Son (e.g. John 4:10; Rom. 6:23), and I think Paul is simply saying that salvation is 'not of [ourselves]; it is the gift of God, not of works, lest anyone should boast'.

As soon as we put our trust in the Lord Jesus Christ, our sins are forgiven, we are made alive spiritually and we have peace with God, but we still struggle with the devil, the sinful world around us and the sinful desires within us. However, we can know a present salvation from these powerful influences by the help of God's grace (Rom. 6:14). Moreover, the Bible also speaks about future salvation. Some things await 'the ages to come' when God will 'show the exceeding riches of His grace in His kindness toward us in Christ Jesus' (Eph. 2:7).

> Amazing grace! how sweet the sound,
> That saved a wretch like me!
> (John Newton)

The certainty of the promise

Most assuredly, I say to you, he who hears My word and believes in Him who sent Me has everlasting life, and shall not come into [condemnation], but has passed from death into life.

(John 5:24)

These words were spoken by the Lord Jesus Christ. Like the words of the apostle Paul in Ephesians 2:8–9, they refer to the gospel promise, the promise of salvation and everlasting life. However, the emphasis this time is on the certainty of the promise.

God does not tell lies. When He says something, we should believe Him. However, God understands us and He is willing to stoop to our level. The Son of God does this by prefacing the promise with the very emphatic words, 'Most assuredly'. The fact that He is speaking should be enough, but He stoops to our level and assures us that we can put our whole trust in what He is saying.

The Lord Jesus Christ says that whoever 'hears My word and believes in Him who sent Me has everlasting life'. Have you heard the message of salvation, and have you believed and trusted in God as the One who sent his Son to be your Saviour? If so, the Lord Jesus says that everlasting life is yours and there is no need to fear condemnation on the Day of Judgement. Already you have 'passed from death into life'. You can be sure because He says so. The Lord says it, and that settles it!

When we want to be sure, we trust in the promise of God, not in feelings. We are sure of salvation because of what God

1 Thirty Sparkling Gems

says in His Word. 'God is not a man, that He should lie' (Num. 23:19). Nothing will make you happier than trusting in the promise of God in His Word.

This was the experience of Ira Sankey, the great American gospel singer and composer (1840–1908). He put his trust in a similar promise in the sixth chapter of John. In his *Addresses on the Gospel of John*, Dr Harry Ironside says:

> I heard Ira D. Sankey tell how he had been anxious for days and months for the assurance of salvation . . . But as he sat in a meeting he was led to turn to this sixth chapter of John and his eyes fell on [the] forty-seventh verse, and it came home to his soul with a strangely new and wonderful meaning, 'He that believeth on Me hath everlasting life' . . . he looked up and said, 'Lord, I believe. I dare to take Thee at Thy word.' And that was the beginning of that great ministry of gospel song to hundreds of thousands of people, carrying the glad message of a full and free salvation.[1]

Christian reader, let this be your experience, and mine too. Let us dare to take God at His Word and then let us go on to be a blessing to many others.

The promise
of friendship

Therefore, having been justified by faith, we have peace with God through our Lord Jesus Christ.

(Rom. 5:1)

The apostle Paul's epistle to the Romans is the fullest and most systematic explanation of the Christian message found anywhere in the Bible and it should be read and understood by every Christian. Martin Luther said that it is 'worthy . . . that every Christian should know it word for word, by heart'. The first four chapters teach:

- the sinfulness of all mankind (e.g. 3:9);
- the impossibility of being 'justified' or declared righteous before God by anything we do (e.g. 3:20);
- justification through what the Lord Jesus Christ accomplished at the Cross, received simply and solely by faith in Him (e.g. 3:24 and 3:28).

Justification is more than forgiveness; it is (to use the well-known explanation) 'just as if I'd never sinned'. Justice has been satisfied because the Lord Jesus paid the price in full at the Cross on behalf of whoever puts their trust in Him. It is a wonderful thing that 'God can save, yet righteous be',[1] and it has wonderful consequences. The first is *peace*, or friendship, with God (5:1). Justice has been satisfied and friendly relations between God and mankind are now possible. God invites us to enter into friendship with Himself by trusting in the Lord Jesus Christ. This is what the apostle Paul refers to as the 'ministry of reconciliation' (see 2 Cor. 5:18–20). What a wonderful thing it is that God is not only our Creator and our Saviour, but also our Friend!

The Lord Jesus is the only way by which lost sinners can come back to God the Father (John 14:6). This is because He is the only Saviour who was able to die for our sins (see 1 Tim. 2:5–6; 1 Peter 3:18a). We cannot come through Muhammad, Buddha, Confucius or even the Virgin Mary! We have peace with God *through* our Lord Jesus Christ.

In his lovely hymn 'I Hear the Words of Love', Horatius Bonar defines peace with God as 'this blood-sealed friendship', and that is what it is. It is worth more than the whole world and everything in it. This is why Christians are exhorted to 'be content with such things as you have' (Heb. 13:5). God is our Friend who has promised never to leave us nor forsake us. We ought to be content! Also, we ought to trust in God with all our heart and say confidently, 'The LORD is my helper' as we face the challenges of life (Heb. 13:6).

> Frail children of dust,
> And feeble as frail,
> In Thee do we trust,
> Nor find Thee to fail;
> Thy mercies how tender,
> How firm to the end,
> Our Maker, Defender,
> Redeemer and Friend!
> (Robert Grant, 'O Worship the King')

The promise for
deep waters

Fear not, for I have redeemed you; I have called you by your name; you are Mine. When you pass through the waters I will be with you; and through the rivers, they shall not overflow you.

(Isa. 43:1b–2a)

In context, this is a promise to the Old Testament people of God, the nation of Israel. However, all such promises of spiritual blessing are equally applicable to Christians today (see Eph. 1:3). This promise assures us that there is no need to fear the future, because we belong to God. When we go through difficult times, He will be with us and help us.

To 'redeem' means to buy back. The Old Testament speaks about the redemption of land and also of people, by someone near of kin. Obviously, the kinsman had to be willing and able to pay the monetary price involved. This foreshadowed and prepared the way for what the New Testament has to say about redemption. Because the Lord Jesus Christ is both God and Man, He was able to become our Kinsman-Redeemer, dying upon Calvary's Cross to pay the price for sin, so that 'whoever [trusts] in Him should not perish but have everlasting life' (John 3:16).

A response of faith and trust is called for before the redemption accomplished at Calvary's Cross becomes effective. God says, 'I have redeemed you; I have called you by your name; you are Mine.' The common call is heard whenever the gospel is proclaimed, but it is only effective when people feel the pull of the Holy Spirit by which God the Father draws us to the Lord Jesus Christ (see John 6:44). This is what it means for God to call us by name; and when we respond by putting our trust in the Lord Jesus Christ, God says, 'you are Mine'.

It is very reassuring to know that we belong to God, but then what happens? Are we 'carried to the skies on flowery beds of ease', as an old hymn puts it?[1] Not at all! Next come the deep waters. These represent the difficult times—the 'many tribulations' through which all Christians must pass on their way to glory (Acts 14:22). At first, the waters may not seem too deep, but soon they turn into rivers that threaten to overflow us—and they would, were it not that God promises to be with us and help us. Of course, He is with us always (Heb. 13:5), but He draws especially near when we go through difficult times, and the promise is 'they shall not overflow you'.

This is why Christians should welcome the difficult times. This sounds a strange thing to say, but if they deepen our Christian experience and bring us closer to God, then they are worth it. This is why the apostle Paul said that he took pleasure in the difficult times—he knew that when he felt weak, he could rely upon God to make him strong (2 Cor. 12:9–10).

> When through the deep waters I cause thee to go,
> The rivers of woe shall not thee overflow;
> For I will be with thee, thy troubles to bless,
> And sanctify to thee thy deepest distress.
> ('K' in Rippon's Selection of Hymns, 'How Firm a Foundation')

The promise of a heavenly home

*In My Father's house are many mansions; if it were not so, I
would have told you. I go to prepare a place for you. And if I go
and prepare a place for you, I will come again and receive you
to Myself; that where I am, there you may be also.*

(John 14:2–3)

What comforting words! And not only to the apostles
in the upper room, but also to every Christian.
The 'Father's house' is heaven, the abode of God, where,
amazingly, there are many 'mansions' or 'dwelling places' for
sinners. Isaiah, conscious of his sinfulness, cried out, 'Woe is
me . . . !' when he had a vision of the glory of God (see Isa. 6:5),
but the wonderful promise before us is that heaven is the home
of all who put their trust in the Lord Jesus Christ. He died for
our sins on the Cross. He rose again on the third day in victory.
Then, after forty days, He was taken up into heaven (see Luke
24:50–51) to prepare a place for us there, and soon He will
come again and receive us to Himself.

When a Christian dies, it is the body that dies—what the
apostle Paul calls the 'outward man'. By contrast, the 'inward
man', the soul, the spirit, is more alive than ever. It goes to
be 'with the Lord'—see 2 Corinthians 4:16 and 5:8. However,
when the Lord Jesus said 'I will come again', He was looking
beyond this to the Second Coming. This is when all Christians
will be 'caught up together' in glorious resurrection bodies 'to
meet the Lord in the air' (see 1 Thes. 4:16–17; Phil. 3:20–21).

After that, we shall always be with Him. When He judges
the world, the devil and the fallen angels, we shall be associated

with Him in that judgement, and when He sits upon His throne in 'the heavenly Jerusalem', we shall serve Him there, we shall see His face and we shall be happy all the days of eternity in the presence of God our Father and the Lord Jesus Christ, 'who died for us, that whether we wake or sleep, we should live together with Him' (see 1 Thes. 5:9–10; Heb. 12:22–24).

The promise of a heavenly home is for all Christians. The words were originally spoken to the apostles, but they were the founder members of the church and the promise is for the whole church. By 'church', I do not mean an organization, but a worldwide spiritual entity composed of all true Christians—that is, all who trust in the Lord Jesus Christ as their Saviour (see Gal. 3:28).

When the apostle Paul wrote to the Christians at Colosse, he said, 'we heard of your faith in Christ Jesus and of your love for all the saints; because of the hope which is laid up for you in heaven' (Col. 1:4–5). They trusted in the Lord Jesus Christ as their Saviour, they loved God, they loved His people and they looked forward to 'the hope which is laid up for you in heaven'. So can every Christian!

> When we all get to Heaven,
> What a day of rejoicing that will be!
> When we all see Jesus,
> We'll sing and shout the victory!
> (E. E. Hewitt, 'Sing the Wondrous Love of Jesus')

The promise that others in our family will be saved

Believe on the Lord Jesus Christ, and you will be saved, you and your household.

(Acts 16:31)

The Bible says that 'he called for a light, ran in, and fell down trembling before Paul and Silas'. Then he brought them out and said, 'Sirs, what must I do to be saved?' (Acts 16:29–30). The trembling man was the Philippian jailer, the rough, tough man who had 'thrust [Paul and Silas] into the inner prison, and made their feet fast in the stocks', ignoring the fact that their backs were badly lacerated from the beating they had both received (see 16:22–24, KJV). An earthquake had woken him from sleep and shaken him to the core of his being.

Those who are in earnest ask the right questions and get the right answers. The jailer was assured that the only thing he had to do was to 'believe on', or trust in, the Lord Jesus Christ (16:31), and 'Then they spoke the word of the Lord to him', no doubt explaining the greatness of the Lord Jesus Christ's Person and Work (16:32). The jailer showed the genuineness of his faith by attending to the wounds of Paul and Silas, and then by being baptized (16:33).

However, in saying all this, I have left one important thing out. The promise of salvation was not to the jailer alone. What Paul and Silas said was, 'you will be saved, you and your household'. The Lord's message was not spoken to the jailer alone, but also 'to all who were in his house' (16:32), and, in response, the whole household believed (see 16:34) and were baptized. God has a particular interest in saving whole families. Commenting on this, the great Victorian preacher Charles Spurgeon said: 'Lord, I would not run away with half a promise when thou dost give a whole one. I beseech thee, save all my family. Save the nearest and dearest. Convert the children, and the grandchildren, if I have any. Be gracious to my servants, and all who dwell under my roof, or work for me.'[1]

I think it is going too far to insist that all such will be saved, but Acts 16:31 certainly leads us to believe that some will be, and it is important that we believe this and pray with confidence for our family—one reason why our prayers are unanswered is lack of faith (see Mark 11:24). We should remember that God has a mighty heart of love. He wants people to be saved, and the words 'Believe on the Lord Jesus Christ, and you will be saved, you and your household' sparkle with hope. For example, in 1 Corinthians 7:12–16, the apostle Paul considers the case of a man or woman who is already married with children when he or she becomes a Christian. He says that the unbelieving spouse is 'sanctified' and the children are 'holy' (7:14). This does not mean that their salvation is guaranteed, but they may well be saved in due course, and this is a good reason not to get a divorce. Also, it is a good reason to pray.

> Pray, pray without ceasing;
> If in your heart you believe,
> Faith shall at length be rewarded,
> You shall the answer receive.
> (E. H. G. Sargent)

The promise that others in our family will be saved

The promise of
daily cleansing

If we confess our sins, He is faithful and just to forgive us our sins and to cleanse us from all unrighteousness.

(1 John 1:9)

The first epistle of John was written to Christians. The reason why Christians sin is because we still have a sinful nature within us. If we say otherwise, 'we deceive ourselves', says the apostle (see 1 John 1:8). Even the saintly apostle still had a sinful nature. Christians want to stop doing evil and start doing good, but there is an enemy within. Victory is possible, but so is defeat.

When Christians sin, we do not lose our salvation, but we do lose the joy of salvation. However, there is a way back. We need to confess our sin or sins to God, as our text says— daily or even immediately, the sooner the better (sometimes it is also right and proper for Christians to confess their sins to one another, but this is not what John is talking about). This means telling God about our sins, saying we are sorry, and asking for His forgiveness and help to forsake those things which have grieved Him. If we do this, God is 'faithful and just to forgive us'. This means that He can be trusted to forgive us and it is right for Him to do this, because justice was satisfied at the Cross when the Lord Jesus Christ 'died for our sins' (1 Cor. 15:3). It is His precious shed blood that 'cleanses us from all sin' (1 John 1:7).

When we first trust in the Lord Jesus Christ as our Saviour, His precious blood cleanses us once and for all from the guilt of sin and we are 'justified', or declared righteous (Rom. 3:24, 28). When Christians sin, we do not lose our righteous standing before God, but sin still defiles us, hinders our fellowship with God (the word 'fellowship' occurs four times in 1 John 1) and robs us of our joy. However, if we confess our sins, He can be trusted 'to forgive us our sins and to cleanse us'. This is the way to get our joy back (see 1 John 1:4), but we must be careful to forsake our sins. God can be trusted to forgive us as soon as we confess them, but confessing and forsaking go together (e.g. Prov. 28:13). Unless we are careful to forsake our sins, we will soon be back in the same defiled, joyless state as before. God will not tolerate sin in the lives of His children. Sin can be confessed and forsaken with God's help, but if we do not do this, God may well permit some painful experience to come into our lives to bring us to our senses. The Bible calls this 'the chastening of the Lord' and says there is a loving purpose in it (see Heb. 12:5–6).

Many of the Christians at Corinth experienced this chastening. In their case, it meant weakness, sickness and even death. Christians who experience God's chastening do not lose their salvation, but the whole thing can be avoided if we 'judge ourselves' by confessing and forsaking our sins (see 1 Cor. 11:30–32).

> Then all is peace and light
> This soul within;
> Thus shall I walk with Thee,
> The Loved unseen,

Leaning on Thee, my God,
Guided along the road,
Nothing between.
(Horatius Bonar, 'No, Not Despairingly')

The promise of
eternal security

And I give [My sheep] eternal life, and they shall never perish; neither shall anyone snatch them out of My hand. My Father, who has given them to Me, is greater than all; and no one is able to snatch them out of My Father's hand.

(John 10:28–29)

The Lord Jesus Christ is 'the good shepherd [who] gives His life for the sheep' (John 10:11), and Christians are His sheep. The Lord says concerning His sheep, 'I give them eternal life.' He gives it to us freely when we put our trust in Him as our Saviour (e.g. John 3:14–15), and we shall never lose it. He says, 'I give them eternal life, and they shall never perish.' This is the promise of eternal security.

When the Bible says 'never', it means 'never'! Christians cannot lose their salvation. This is because the Lord Jesus holds onto us, and His grip is stronger than sin and the devil, who try to snatch us out of His hand. God the Father holds onto us, too, and it is impossible for anyone to snatch us out of His hand. The Father and the Son are essentially one, and they are one in their love for those who trust in the Lord Jesus Christ (see John 10:30). This means that, if we really do trust in the Lord Jesus Christ, we cannot lose our salvation. Theologians sometimes refer to this teaching as the doctrine of eternal security. Once saved, always saved.

For example, the apostle Peter denied his Lord three times with oaths and curses and this was a very serious failure, but the Lord Jesus Christ prayed for him that his faith should not fail (see Luke 22:32) and, of course, God the Father heard His prayer and Peter's faith did not fail. The Lord Jesus still prays for those who trust in Him. The Bible says that He is 'at the right hand of God' where He 'makes intercession for us' (Rom. 8:34). This is why we are eternally secure—because the Lord Jesus Christ loves us and intercedes for us.

God the Father loves us too. It was He who loved the world so much that He gave His only Son (see John 3:16). This love of God which is in Christ Jesus our Lord is the strongest thing in the world. Nothing can separate us from it. In Romans 8:35, the apostle Paul throws out the challenge: 'Who shall separate us from the love of Christ?' Shall the difficult times that all Christians go through? Or how about the fierce persecution that some Christians have to face? 'No!' says Paul; 'in all these things we are more than conquerors through him who loved us' (Rom. 8:37, RSV). The love of God holds onto us through it all and enables us to triumph at last. The apostle assures us that there is nothing, nothing, nothing that is able 'to separate us from the love of God which is in Christ Jesus our Lord' (see Rom. 8:38–39).

> Jesus my Lord will love me for ever,
> From Him no pow'r of evil can sever,
> He gave His life to ransom my soul;
> Now I belong to Him:
>
> *Now I belong to Jesus,*
> *Jesus belongs to me,*
> *Not for the years of time alone,*
> *But for eternity.*
> (Norman J. Clayton)

The promise of strength when needed

As your days, so shall your strength be.

(Deut. 33:25b)

In Deuteronomy 33, we find 'the blessing with which Moses the man of God blessed the children of Israel before his death' (Deut. 33:1). One of the promises given to the tribe of Asher was 'As your days, so shall your strength be.' All such promises of spiritual blessing are equally applicable to Christians today. God gives us extra strength when we need it.

This was the apostle Paul's experience. He had a 'thorn in the flesh' (see 2 Cor. 12:7–9). We are not told precisely what this was, but it obviously made life difficult for him and he prayed earnestly for its removal. His prayer was answered, but instead of the 'thorn' being removed, Paul was assured that God's grace and strength would be sufficient for him. God would give him extra strength when he needed it, and Paul's weakness was an opportunity for God's strength to be displayed. Consequently, Paul was able to say, 'I can do all things through Christ who strengthens me' (Phil. 4:13). If we are Christians, we can say the same. The same Lord Jesus Christ who strengthened Paul can strengthen us.

Of course, we are expected to be sensible. If we are tired, we should go to bed early, and if we need a holiday, we should take one. However, there are times when it is not possible, or at least not right, to go on holiday or even to go to bed early. For example, in the Garden of Gethsemane, Simon Peter, James and John were very tired and went to sleep, but they should have been watching and praying (see Matt. 26:36–41). In such cases, Christians can pray to God for the extra strength they need, claiming the promise to the tribe of Asher.

I find this promise of strength when needed very reassuring. Do you ever worry about the future? Your Christian life is OK at the moment, but what if this happens or what if that happens? We are weak in and of ourselves, but God promises that the strength He gives us will always be enough. He will not allow us to be tempted beyond what we are able to bear (see 1 Cor. 10:13). We should trust Him and live one day at a time.

One reason why worry is bad is because it saps the strength we ought to be giving to the present. The Lord Jesus Christ concluded His teaching about worry in the Sermon on the Mount by saying, 'Sufficient for the day is its own trouble' (Matt. 6:34). The demands of each day are enough. God gives us the strength to cope with them, as the promise of strength when needed assures us, but He does not give us the strength to worry as well. This does not preclude thinking ahead and making sensible provision for the future, but it does preclude thinking ahead in an unbelieving, distrustful way. Let us live one day at a time and trust in our Heavenly Father.

> In every condition—in sickness, in health,
> In poverty's vale, or abounding in wealth;
> At home or abroad, on the land, on the sea,
> As days may demand, shall thy strength ever be.
> ('How Firm a Foundation')

The promise of strength when needed

The promise
of guidance

I will instruct you and teach you in the way you should go; I will guide you with My eye.

(Ps. 32:8)

Often in the Christian life we know what we ought to be doing and the only problem is doing it. However, at times there is another problem: we do not know what we ought to be doing. If we are Christians, then God is our Heavenly Father and at such times He promises to 'instruct [us] and teach [us] in the way [we] should go'. He promises to 'guide [us] with [His] eye'. This could mean that He promises to 'keep an eye on us', as we might say, and give us timely guidance, if we are in danger of going astray. Alternatively, it could mean that 'As servants take their cue from the master's eye . . . so should we obey the slightest hints of our Master'.[1]

However, we cannot expect God to instruct us and teach us and guide us if we keep our Bibles shut. God has given us His Word so that we may be 'thoroughly equipped for every good work' (2 Tim. 3:16–17), and He expects us to read it! Christians who are perplexed about what they ought to be doing often find that their daily Bible readings are very appropriate and give them timely guidance. The Bible can make us wise enough to tackle difficult decisions, especially when our Bible reading is combined with earnest prayer (see James 1:5).

Guidance is a big subject. Something should be said about the providence of God. This refers to the ways by which God exerts control over all things, preserving and governing all His creatures and all their actions. God's knowledge and control extend to the smallest of His creatures (e.g. Matt. 10:29) and the most insignificant details of our lives (e.g. Matt. 10:30).

Something should also be said about the special guidance that God sometimes gives. In such cases, there is no need to weigh up the pros and cons, because the guidance is so clear and unmistakable. I deal with both providential guidance and special guidance at some length in my book *What Happens When . . . ?* published by Day One; see the chapter entitled 'When Christians Are Perplexed'.

However, the problem sometimes is that Christians do not feel their need of guidance. This is why the psalmist, King David, goes on to speak about the horse and the mule (see Ps. 32:9). Some Christians gallop off like horses without waiting for further instruction, whereas others are as stubborn as mules and refuse to be guided by God's Word. In such cases, God adopts a rougher method—the 'bit and bridle' of divine chastening. Let us be like neither, but humbly seek the guidance which God has promised to His children.

> Teach me Thy way, O Lord,
> Teach me Thy way;
> Thy gracious aid afford,
> Teach me Thy way;
> Help me to walk aright,
> More by faith, less by sight;

Lead me with heavenly light:
Teach me Thy way.
(Benjamin Mansell Ramsey)

The promise
of provision

And my God shall supply all your need according to His riches in glory by Christ Jesus.

(Phil. 4:19)

When considering any of the promises of God, we should always bear in mind to whom the promise is made, and what conditions, if any, apply. For example, the gospel promise (John 3:16) is made to the whole wide world and the condition is trusting in the Lord Jesus Christ as Saviour, whereas the promise of daily cleansing (1 John 1:9) is made to those who are already Christians and the condition is confessing our sins to God.

The promise we are considering here was originally made to the Christians at Philippi, and to them it was unconditional. However, I think we do well to take a closer look at what sort of Christians those Christians at Philippi were. They were the sort of Christians whose love was genuine and practical. They knew that the apostle Paul was often in need as he travelled far and wide preaching the gospel, and they 'sent aid once and again for [his] necessities' (Phil. 4:16). Even when he was in prison in Rome, they found a way of doing this, by sending Epaphroditus with the wherewithal to minister to Paul's need. Commenting on this, Geoffrey Wilson says that 'God is no man's debtor, and He will not fail to supply the needs of those who gladly make sacrifices to forward His cause in the world' (see also Matt. 6:33).[1]

God promises to supply all our need—this includes our

material need and also our spiritual need. Also, he promises to supply our need in a kingly way—'according to His riches in glory by Christ Jesus'. Therefore we should not fear to make our needs known at the Throne of Grace. As an old hymn puts it:

> Thou art coming to a King,
> Large petitions with thee bring;
> For His grace and power are such,
> None can ever ask too much.
> (John Newton, 'Come, My Soul, Thy Suit Prepare')

The promises of God are of such great worth because they are backed by Almighty God Himself and 'His riches in glory by Christ Jesus'. This means that His resources are vast and glorious, and that they are available to us in and through the Lord Jesus Christ. We are sinners who do not deserve anything good from God, but, trusting in the Lord Jesus Christ as our Saviour, we can come to the Throne of Grace with confidence.

Of course, it should be said that God promises to give us what we need, not what we want. He may not make us rich materially, but we will have enough. It may well not be good for us to have too much. 'Here little, and hereafter bliss, is best from age to age,' says John Bunyan in *The Pilgrim's Progress*.

> The birds, without barn
> Or storehouse, are fed;
> From them let us learn
> To trust for our bread:
> His saints what is fitting

Shall ne'er be denied,
So long as 'tis written,
'The Lord will provide.'
(John Newton, 'Though Troubles Assail Us')

The promise of
a resurrection
body

*For our citizenship is in heaven, from which we also eagerly
wait for the Savior, the Lord Jesus Christ, who will transform
our lowly body that it may be conformed to His glorious body.*

(Phil. 3:20–21a)

When Christians die, we are 'absent from the body
and . . . present with the Lord' (2 Cor. 5:8), but this is
not permanent. It is what theologians call 'the intermediate
state'. Men and women are meant to have bodies, and one
of the fundamental truths in which Christians believe is the
resurrection of the body. Christians who have died are said to
have 'fallen asleep' (e.g. 1 Thes. 4:13). The soul, the spirit, is
alive and happy in heaven. It is the body that 'sleeps' until the
day of resurrection.

The resurrection of the body will take place when the Lord
Jesus Christ comes again. He will 'wake up' the bodies of His
people 'with a shout, with the voice of an archangel, and with
the trumpet of God' (1 Thes. 4:16). Then Christians will be
clothed with bodies once more, but they will be very different
bodies, changed so as to be well suited to the everlasting life
ahead of us. The Bible says that, when the Lord Jesus Christ
comes again, He will 'transform our lowly body that it may be
conformed to His glorious body'.

'Christ died for our sins . . . He was buried . . . He rose
again the third day,' says the Bible (1 Cor. 15:3–4). When the
apostles Peter and John ran to the tomb, they found that it
was empty. The graveclothes were still there, but the body had

gone (see John 20:4–8). Later, the Lord Jesus appeared to his apostles and proved to them that He was indeed alive and had a real and glorious resurrection body. One day, we shall have such a body, too!

Christians are declared righteous the moment we put our trust in the Lord Jesus Christ as our Saviour, simply and solely because of what He did for us on the Cross. This is the start of the Christian life, but the goal is 'the resurrection from the dead' (Phil. 3:11), when we shall enter into our salvation in all its fullness.

The way Christians attain to this varies. Some nobly die a martyr's death, others glorify God by means of a long life of Christian service, and yet others will not die at all because they will still be alive here on the earth when Jesus comes again. But whatever our route to the Glory may be, our arrival is a certainty. So long as we start at Calvary's Cross by genuinely putting our trust in the Lord Jesus Christ as our Saviour, our arrival in the Glory is a certainty—the Bible says 'whom He justified, these He also glorified' (Rom. 8:30).

> The heavens shall glow with splendour;
> But brighter far than they,
> The saints shall shine in glory,
> As Christ shall them array:
> The beauty of the Saviour
> Shall dazzle every eye,
> In the crowning day that's coming
> By and by.
> (El Nathan, 'Our Lord Is Now Rejected')

The promise of the Second Coming

Men of Galilee, why do you stand gazing up into heaven?
This same Jesus, who was taken up from you into heaven, will
so come in like manner as you saw Him go into heaven.

(Acts 1:11)

While his apostles watched, the Lord Jesus Christ 'was taken up, and a cloud received Him out of their sight' (Acts 1:9). Then two angelic messengers stood by them in human form and gave them this wonderful promise of the Second Coming of 'this same Jesus'. The same wonderful Person who is set forth in the four Gospels, the same wonderful Saviour who died for our sins, was buried and rose again the third day—He is the One who is coming again.

And His coming will be 'in like manner as you saw Him go'. This means that His coming will be personal and visible—those who are alive and remain on that day 'will see the Son of Man coming on the clouds of heaven with power and great glory' (Matt. 24:30). 'Every eye will see Him' (Rev. 1:7). What a great joy it will be to those who are trusting in Him as their Saviour! But what consternation it will cause to an unbelieving world!

And what a truly awesome event the Second Coming will be. The whole universe will be shaken by it. The apostle John was given a vision of the future and he tells us that

> there was a great earthquake; and the sun became
> black as sackcloth of hair, and the moon became like
> blood. And the stars of heaven fell to the earth, as a

fig tree drops its late figs when it is shaken by a mighty wind. Then the sky receded as a scroll when it is rolled up, and every mountain and island was moved out of its place. (Rev. 6:12–14)

Of course, many people scoff at all this and say Christians have been talking about the Second Coming for almost two thousand years and the Lord Jesus Christ still has not come back. Why has there been such a long delay? The Bible gives a clear answer: 'The Lord is not slack concerning His promise, as some count slackness, but is longsuffering toward us, not willing that any should perish but that all should come to repentance' (2 Peter 3:9). God is waiting patiently so that more people can 'come to repentance' and be saved. 'But the day of the Lord will come' (2 Peter 3:10a). God is not going to wait for ever.

> Another day, another year,
> The coming of the Lord draws near;
> The day for which the Christian longs—
> The day of days when all the wrongs,
> At last, shall be put right.
>
> We then shall our Redeemer see
> And everyone will bow the knee
> And every tongue confess His name:
> The Lord of Glory who once came
> To save us from our sins.

Our Lord and Saviour died and rose
And won the victory o'er His foes;
The devil's kingdom soon will fall;
Jesus will come and reign o'er all;
Oh, that it were today!

Why does the Lord delay so long,
When grief is great and much is wrong?
He is not slack the Bible says,
But waits for us, from sinful ways
To turn, while yet we may.

Soon, soon, will come the Prince of Peace;
Soon, soon, creation's groans will cease;
We soon will hear the Bridegroom's voice;
Soon, those who love Him will rejoice;
Be ready, when He comes!
(Peter Currie)

The promise of an elect company and a warm welcome

All that the Father gives Me will come to Me, and the one who comes to Me I will by no means cast out.

(John 6:37)

These words were spoken to the Jewish people who lived in Galilee. In general, these people were more positive towards the Lord Jesus Christ than those who lived in Jerusalem and Judea, and many of His mighty miracles were done in this region. However, the problem with most of the Galileans was simply their lack of genuine saving faith (see John 6:35–36). Nevertheless, in this promise that we are considering, the Lord Jesus assured them that some people *would* come to Him and put their trust in Him and that there was a warm welcome for anyone who did thus come. It is God's will and purpose that there should be such a people, composed of whoever trusts in His Son, who have everlasting spiritual life even now, and who will be raised up at the end of time to enjoy the fullness of the wonderful things that God has in store for them (see John 6:38–40).

This company of people is sometimes referred to as 'the elect' (e.g. Matt. 24:22–24, 31). The Bible says that Christians are 'elect according to the foreknowledge of God the Father' (1 Peter 1:2a). We were given to the Lord Jesus Christ before the dawn of time. The salvation of the elect is a certainty because the Lord Jesus promises that the elect '*will* come to Me'. There is no doubt about it! *This is the promise of an elect company.*

The doctrine of election is an awe-inspiring doctrine, but it can also be a chilling doctrine if mishandled. I think this is why the Lord Jesus Christ immediately added that 'the one who comes to Me I will by no means cast out'. This saying is very emphatic. It could be translated 'the one who comes to Me I will *most certainly not* cast out' (Amplified Bible, emphasis added). *This is the promise of a warm welcome* and it comes from a mighty heart of love which 'desires all men to be saved and to come to the knowledge of the truth' (1 Tim. 2:3–4). I believe this means all people without exception, just as Jesus commanded that the gospel should be proclaimed to all people without exception (see Mark 16:15).

John Bunyan certainly believed in the doctrine of election but he rejoiced in this promise of a warm welcome as well. In his immortal allegory *The Pilgrim's Progress*, when Christian comes to the Wicket Gate he is told, 'We make no objections against any notwithstanding all they have done before they come hither. They in no wise are cast out.'

Some Christians emphasize the doctrine of election and play down the truth of God's love for the whole wide world, while others emphasize the truth of God's love for the whole wide world and play down the doctrine of election. However, both are in the Bible and we should believe both. They may seem like parallel lines which never meet, but the Lord Jesus Christ brought these truths together very simply in this promise that we are considering. He affirms the doctrine of election by saying, 'All that the Father gives Me will come to Me', but then our gracious Lord and Saviour immediately adds that 'the one who comes to Me I will by no means cast out'. This is the truth of God's love for the whole wide world.

Becoming a Christian is like coming to a door over which are the words 'The one who comes to Me I will by no means cast out.' On the strength of this promise we go through the door, rejoicing that there is such a warm welcome for sinners. Then, having gone through the door, we look back and on the other side of the door we see the words 'All that the Father gives Me will come to Me', and we are amazed to discover that we were among that foreknown, elect company who were given to the Lord Jesus Christ before the dawn of time. As Dr Harry Ironside so aptly says, these things are 'not for theologians to wrangle over but for saints to rejoice in'.[1]

The promise of
a willing Guest

Behold, I stand at the door and knock. If anyone hears My voice and opens the door, I will come in to him and dine with him, and he with Me.

(Rev. 3:20)

The book of Revelation contains many promises. This is one, and we will be looking at some others later on. The book begins with a vision of the Lord Jesus Christ in the midst of 'the seven churches which are in Asia' (Rev. 1:4a). This is followed in chapters 2 and 3 by a special message to each of these churches.

The seven churches were different from one another, and it may well be that every local church that has ever existed can find itself in one of these churches. Two of the churches receive unqualified praise: suffering Smyrna and faithful Philadelphia. However, others had problems: Ephesus was hard working, but it was not a labour of love as it used to be; Pergamos had become a bit careless and they were tolerating things that should not be tolerated; Thyatira had a big problem with a woman who claimed to be 'a prophetess' (2:20); and Sardis had a big problem with nominal Christianity.

Finally, we come to Laodicea, to whom the promise that we are considering was originally spoken. The problem with this church was lukewarmness, half-heartedness, a lack of zeal— yet they themselves felt that all was well! But where was the Lord Jesus Christ? In the midst? No, He was outside the door, knocking to be let in, as our verse says! Probably most of the church members were not truly converted, but still the Lord Jesus, though sickened by their lukewarmness, graciously sought admission to any heart that was willing to repent and receive Him.

There is a famous picture painted by William Holman Hunt which illustrates our promise. It shows the Lord Jesus Christ preparing to knock on an overgrown and long-unopened door. The door in the painting has no handle, and can therefore be opened only from the inside, representing 'the obstinately shut mind', as Hunt put it.[1] However, the Lord Jesus makes His presence felt by knocking on the door. This represents what happens when the gospel is proclaimed 'in power, and in the Holy Spirit and in much assurance' (1 Thes. 1:5a). This explains why the Lord refers to the knocking as 'My voice'.

When we respond, by trusting in the Lord Jesus Christ as our Saviour, this is how we open the door, and when we do so, the Lord Jesus promises to come in. There are no exceptions—'if anyone hears My voice and opens the door, I will come in to him'. It is a promise, and it is followed by fellowship—'I will come in to him and dine with him, and he with Me.' A meal is a time when people relax and talk, and it is a fitting symbol of the fellowship, the friendship, with the Lord Jesus Christ that Christians enjoy both now and in eternity.

> O Lord, in my heart there's a welcome for Thee.
> Gladly I now would say,
> Come in, blessed Saviour, my heart and my life
> Henceforth would own Thy sway.

Long hast Thou waited and long knocked in vain
Outside my heart's closed door;
Oh, cleanse me from sin, then, dear Lord, enter in
And dwell there for evermore.
(H. M. Day, 'No Room for the Baby at Bethlehem's Inn')

THE BEATITUDES

The Sermon on the Mount is one of the best-known passages of the Bible. But it is also one of the most frequently misunderstood. The best place to begin is, of course, at the beginning, and what a beginning it is: eight wonderful 'Beatitudes', pronouncements which promise particular blessings to people who possess particular characteristics—see Matthew 5:1–12. We will consider the meaning of these wonderful promises in a series of eight meditations, and my prayer is that it will indeed be a blessing to those who read it and take to heart its message.

The promise to
the poor in spirit

Blessed are the poor in spirit, for theirs is the kingdom of heaven.

(Matt. 5:3)

Our text is the first Beatitude. Its promise is comprehensive and the required characteristic is fundamental. The 'kingdom of heaven' means the wonderful 'kingdom prepared . . . from the foundation of the world' for God's people (Matt. 25:34). The full manifestation of this glorious kingdom awaits the return of the Lord Jesus Christ at His Second Coming (see Luke 19:11–12). All who are truly 'poor in spirit' belong to this kingdom even now (see Col. 1:12–14) and, when the Lord comes again, they shall enjoy the fullness of its blessings. This prompts us to ask a number of questions:

- What does it mean to be poor in spirit?
- Why is it so important?
- How do we become poor in spirit?
- How does this fit in with the gospel promises to those who trust in the Lord Jesus Christ as their Saviour?

The problem with riches is that they tend to make us feel self-sufficient. The world encourages people to be self-sufficient and believe in themselves, but to be poor in spirit is the opposite. It is to say with Paul, 'And who is sufficient for these things?' (2 Cor. 2:16b). It makes us feel our need of God and of His grace (see 2 Cor. 3:5; 12:9a). If this is our attitude, then we are poor in spirit, whether we are rich or poor in material terms.

No one ever becomes a Christian without being poor in spirit. This is why it is so important. We have to be convinced of our spiritual poverty before we will ever accept the gospel remedy. Faith is the only condition of salvation, but we will never put our faith and trust in the Lord Jesus Christ until we feel our need of Him. This is why the law was given to Israel through Moses at Mount Sinai. God knew that they would not be able to keep it; His purpose was to show them that they were sinners in need of a Saviour—to make them poor in spirit (see Rom. 3:20).

My mother took me to church when I was a small boy, as I said in the very first meditation of this book. However, it was only when I went to hear Dr Billy Graham that I knew what it was to be poor in spirit. Suddenly, I felt so much that I needed the Saviour of whom he was speaking, and it was not long before I had been led to put my trust in Him.

> Just as I am, without one plea,
> But that Thy blood was shed for me,
> And that Thou bidd'st me come to Thee,
> O Lamb of God, I come.
>
> Just as I am, and waiting not
> To rid my soul of one dark blot,
> To Thee, whose blood can cleanse each spot,
> O Lamb of God, I come.
>
> Just as I am, poor, wretched, blind;
> Sight, riches, healing of the mind,

Yea, all I need, in Thee to find,
O Lamb of God, I come.
(Charlotte Elliott)

The promise to those who mourn

Blessed are those who mourn, for they shall be comforted.

(Matt. 5:4)

As we go through the Beatitudes, I think we will see that they are in a logical order. This is certainly true of the first two—if we recognize our spiritual poverty, we will mourn over it, we will be sorry about it.

Sorrow for sin occurs both before and after someone becomes a Christian, and it is very precious. In his book *The Chemistry of the Blood*, Dr M. R. De Haan writes:

> The story is told of the angel who was sent to earth with orders to bring back the most precious thing he could find on earth. He flew down and searched from pole to pole. He delved into the bowels of the earth and explored the depths of the sea and the wonders of the air. He picked up a gold nugget, but as he looked upon it, he said, 'No! No! This is not good enough for the King!' He gathered a handful of the most precious diamonds, but halfway to heaven he stopped and blushed and turned back to earth. He sought and sought, but nothing seemed precious enough. And then, while he stood musing in a glen, he heard a sob. He looked up and saw a sinner kneeling on a rock, and with drooping head, pouring out his heart to God for pardon and forgiveness. Even as he prayed, the tears started and fell down before the unseen angel. 'Ah!' said the heavenly messenger, 'I have found it,' and

holding a golden chalice under the rock, he caught one penitent tear and flew back in triumph to heaven and God, with the most precious thing on all the earth.[1]

I ought to qualify this by saying that not all sorrow for sin is precious; not all leads to blessing. The mark of genuine sorrow for sin is that it produces repentance—a change of attitude leading to a change of behaviour (see 2 Cor. 7:10). The story is told of a little girl whose brother was unkind to her. Later on he said sorry, but she was not satisfied. She asked him, 'What kind of sorry, the kind of sorry that you won't do it again?'

Returning to our text, this idea of mourning and being comforted is rooted in the Old Testament. For example, the prophet Isaiah predicted that the Messiah would 'comfort all who mourn' (see Isa. 61:1–2). In fact, the prophet has a lot to say about the subject. For example, he says that the mourning goes beyond being sorry about our own sins and includes being sorry about the sins of others (see 66:10 where he speaks about 'all you who mourn for [Jerusalem]'; even the sinless Son of God mourned in this sense—see Luke 19:41). As for the comfort promised, it includes the forgiveness of sins (see Isa. 40:1–2) and also looks ahead to the time when God will banish every consequence of sin from the new earth (see 51:3 which says that 'He will make [His people's] wilderness like Eden and [their] desert like the garden of the LORD').

This is the promise to those who mourn, but the question is, do we qualify? Do we mourn? Yes, Christians should be cheerful because of the forgiveness of sins and hopeful as we look ahead,

but there should be a serious side to our Christianity as well—
'sorrowful, yet always rejoicing' (2 Cor. 6:10a).

The promise
to the meek

Blessed are the meek, for they shall inherit the earth.

(Matt. 5:5)

Meekness is not a virtue admired by the world. The world applauds those who assert themselves and thrust themselves forward, whereas a meek person is reluctant to do this. The Greek word translated 'meek' means someone who is mild-tempered and humble. Meekness and humility are closely related.

The world thinks that meekness is weakness, but this is not the case. It is strength under control. Moses was a great leader of God's people and yet the Bible says that he was very meek (Num. 12:3, KJV). David was a man of war, chosen by God to replace Saul as king, but, even though he knew this, he did not thrust himself forward. Twice he could have killed Saul, but he did not—he was meek (see 1 Sam. 24:1–7; 26:1–11).

The perfect example of meekness is our Lord Jesus Christ, who said of Himself: 'I am meek and lowly in heart' (Matt. 11:29, KJV). Because he was like this, He was willing to leave all the glory of heaven and come down—down to earth, down to Manhood, down to the Cross (see Phil. 2:5–8). What condescension! What meekness!

Some people are naturally mild-tempered, but Christian meekness goes beyond this. It is part of the fruit of the Spirit (see Gal. 5:22–23, KJV; the Greek word for the eighth part of the fruit is derived from a form of the Greek word used in Matt. 5:5) and it follows on logically from the first two Beatitudes: if we recognize our spiritual poverty and mourn over it, then we will have a humble opinion of ourselves and we will not be too upset if others point out our faults.

Becoming a Christian is a humbling experience. God 'brings low' before he 'lifts up' (see 1 Sam. 2:6–8). He shows us that we are good-for-nothing hell-deserving sinners before He draws us to the Saviour. However, there is still a lot of pride in us, even after we become Christians, and there are times when God needs to bring us low. If this is our experience, let us learn to be more humble, knowing that 'God resists the proud, but gives grace to the humble' (1 Peter 5:5b).

Much is promised to those who are humble and meek. One day they 'shall inherit the earth'! Like the second Beatitude, this promise is rooted in the Old Testament—see Psalm 37:11. The meaning is that although evildoers may prosper for a time, 'they shall soon be cut down like the grass' (see 37:1–2) and then 'the meek [in the end] shall inherit the earth' (37:11, Amplified Bible, Classic Edition). This will be fulfilled at the Second Coming of our Lord Jesus Christ—this is when 'the saints of the Most High shall receive the kingdom, and possess the kingdom forever, even forever and ever' (Dan. 7:18; see also Rev. 22:5).

Of course, the world scoffs at the idea of the Second Coming. It says that the assertive and proud are the ones who will inherit the earth—people like the great Roman, Julius Caesar, who famously said, 'I came, I saw, I conquered.' He wanted to bring an end to the Roman Republic and thrust himself forward as emperor. However, it was not long before he was 'cut down like the grass', and this will be the end of all the great ones of this world, in the end—unless they repent and put their trust in the Lord Jesus Christ while it is still the day of grace (see Ps. 2:10–12).

The promise to those who hunger and thirst for righteousness

Blessed are those who hunger and thirst for righteousness, for they shall be filled.

(Matt. 5:6)

The first three Beatitudes set forth negative characteristics—a recognition of our spiritual poverty, mourning over sin, and meekness. There is nothing wrong with this—it is very important; but now we move to something positive: a longing for righteousness.

In the Bible, righteousness means two things. It means either right behaviour or being right with God. However, we cannot become right with God by right behaviour. This is because our best efforts to please God by what we do are defiled by sin (see Rom. 3:20; Isa. 64:6a).

The only way to be right with God is by trusting in the Lord Jesus Christ and Him crucified (see Rom. 3:21–26). Moses understood this, albeit dimly, when he wrote Genesis (see Gen. 15:6), Habakkuk understood this when he wrote the book that bears his name (see Hab. 2:4) and the Lord Jesus understood this perfectly when He spoke the words of our text. Those who long to be right with God will be 'filled', or satisfied, when they trust in the Lord Jesus Christ as their Saviour. The Bible says that if we come to the Lord Jesus and put our trust in Him, we shall never 'hunger' or 'thirst' (John 6:35). Some people think that satisfaction is obtained by trying to enjoy what life has to offer or by getting lots of money and possessions, but true satisfaction is found in the Lord Jesus Christ, and a Christian never needs to look elsewhere (see also Jer. 2:13).

When we become Christians, God satisfies our longing to be right with Him. He gives us a new standing—we are declared righteous because of what the Lord Jesus did for us at Calvary's Cross. However, God also gives us a new desire to do what is right (see Rom. 7:22). This is what Christians are like—they hunger and thirst for right behaviour. However, we do not attain to this without a struggle, because the old sinful desires are still within us as well (see Gal. 5:17). Full satisfaction awaits the Second Coming of the Lord Jesus Christ. Then we, together with all God's people, will be 'holy and without blemish' (see Eph. 5:25–27), but until then we must always be pressing on, seeking to make progress in the Christian life (see Phil. 3:12–14).

Let us make sure that we really are hungering and thirsting. These words imply an intensity of desire, a longing. I think I always want to do what is right, but I am not so sure that I always *long* to. Sometimes the 'fleshly lusts which war against the soul' (1 Peter 2:11) seem to take the edge off my spiritual appetite. I suppose it is like when we were children and we were warned not to eat sweets before a meal. We need to avoid anything that will encourage the old sinful desires within us (see Rom. 13:14).

> More holiness give me,
> More striving within;
> More patience in suffering,

More sorrow for sin;
More faith in my Saviour,
More sense of His care;
More joy in His service,
More purpose in prayer.

More gratitude give me,
More trust in the Lord;
More pride in His glory,
More hope in His Word;
More tears for His sorrows,
More pain at His grief;
More meekness in trial,
More praise for relief.

More purity give me,
More strength to o'ercome;
More freedom from earth stains,
More longings for home;
More fit for the kingdom,
More used would I be,
More blessed and holy,
More, Saviour, like Thee!
(P. P. Bliss)

The promise to
the merciful

Blessed are the merciful, for they shall obtain mercy.

(Matt. 5:7)

Mercy is important. The Old Testament emphasizes this by saying that the main things God requires of His people are 'to do justly, to love mercy, and to walk humbly with your God' (Micah 6:8). This is where the scribes and Pharisees went wrong. They were scrupulous as regards outward religious observances, but they had no heart for sinners. They were not merciful (see Matt. 9:9–13).

In his book *Studies in the Sermon on the Mount*, Dr Martyn Lloyd-Jones defines mercy as 'a sense of pity plus a desire to relieve the suffering'[1]—not only a sense of pity, but also a desire to do something about it. The Good Samaritan in the famous parable was like this. Not only did he see the poor man who had been badly treated and feel sorry for him, but he also went to him and did something about it (see Luke 10:30–35).

Dr Lloyd-Jones goes on to say that the supreme example is God Himself. This is why God sent His Son to be our Saviour. In God there is a great hatred of sin, but there is also great mercy. As Dr Martin Luther put it:

> Then was the Father troubled sore
> To see me ever languish.
> The Everlasting Pity swore
> To save me from my anguish.
> He turned to me His father-heart

> And chose Himself a bitter part,
>
> His Dearest did it cost Him.
>
> ('Dear Christians, One and All, Rejoice')

We 'obtain mercy' as soon as we believe and trust in the Lord Jesus Christ as our Saviour. This was true for the apostle Paul and it is true for all believers (see 1 Tim. 1:15–16). Then, having obtained mercy, the Bible says that we should treat others in the same way that God has treated us (e.g. Eph. 4:32).

At first sight, our text seems to contradict this, but this is to misunderstand the Beatitudes. They do not set forth eight conditions of salvation. Rather, they set forth eight characteristics of those who are saved through faith in the Lord Jesus Christ. It is God who works in us, both at conversion and afterwards, to make us like this.

However, we do not attain to this without a struggle, because the old sinful desires are still within us as well. It is possible for Christians to become somewhat hard and unmerciful and, if this happens, God is grieved and our fellowship with Him is hindered (see Eph. 4:30–32). We do not lose our salvation (see John 10:28–29), but we do forfeit the ongoing mercy and help that we need in the Christian life (see Matt. 6:14–15; Heb. 4:16).

If we find ourselves becoming like this, let us remember that anything we are called upon to forgive is a little thing compared to the great mercy that has been shown to us (see Matt. 18:21–35, where the Lord Jesus told a story about a man who was forgiven an enormous debt, but who then refused to forgive a relatively small, though not inconsiderable, debt).

> My song is love unknown,
> My Saviour's love to me,
> Love to the loveless shown,
> That they might lovely be.
> O who am I,
> That for my sake
> My Lord should take
> Frail flesh and die?
> (Samuel Crossman)

The promise to
the pure in heart

Blessed are the pure in heart, for they shall see God.

(Matt. 5:8)

This is a very great saying, and a whole book could be written about it. It goes to the heart of the matter and speaks of the highest good. However, the first thing I want to do is to put this promise to the pure and holy in heart in context.

The fourth Beatitude (the promise to those who hunger and thirst for righteousness) speaks about the positive longing for righteousness which is satisfied to some extent by God justifying us by grace through faith in the Lord Jesus Christ. Mercy and holiness flow from this. We are merciful because God has been merciful to us. We want to be holy because God gives us new desires as well as a new standing.

Our text shows that the Beatitudes are not conditions of salvation. They are not things we can do without God's gracious intervention in our lives. How can any of us be pure and holy in heart apart from this? It is impossible! We are sinners! Rotten to the core! We can attain to an outward hypocritical holiness such as Pharisees might have, but not heart-holiness (see Matt. 23:25–28).

It is only when we trust in the Lord Jesus Christ as our Saviour that our hearts are purified (see Acts 15:7–9). His precious blood cleanses us once and for all from the guilt of sin. Also, as I have said before, we want to be holy. We seek to 'pursue . . . holiness, without which no one will see the Lord'

(Heb. 12:14). It is no use saying we are Christians if we have no interest in being holy. The Bible says that the Lord Jesus Christ is now progressively sanctifying His already justified church so that one day 'He might present her to Himself a glorious church, not having spot or wrinkle or any such thing, but that she should be holy and without blemish' (see Eph. 5:25–27).

How should we go about pursuing holiness? Should we withdraw from the world and go and live in a monastery? No! Our task is to 'go into all the world and preach the gospel to every creature' (Mark 16:15). We go into the world with God's Word and it is the Word that protects us. In His great intercessory prayer, the Lord Jesus Christ said: 'I do not pray that You should take them out of the world, but that You should keep them from the evil one . . . Sanctify them by Your truth. Your word is truth' (John 17:15, 17). The means God uses in our sanctification is His Word, the Bible:

> In my heart, in my heart,
> Send a great revival;
> Teach me how to watch and pray
> And to read the Bible.
> (Anonymous)

All that is needed to make us 'complete, thoroughly equipped for every good work' is contained therein (see 2 Tim. 3:14–17).

The promise to the pure and holy in heart is that 'they shall see God'. To some extent this is true now. For example, we see God when we look around at the wonderful creation He has made (see Rom. 1:20). Better still, we see God when we hear the story of Jesus, because the Lord Jesus is 'the brightness of His glory and the express image of His Person' (Heb. 1:3a; see also John 14:9). However, something far greater awaits us in the future. The Bible says that 'now we see in a mirror, dimly, but then face to face' (1 Cor. 13:12).

> Face to face with Christ my Saviour,
> Face to face—what will it be
> When with rapture I behold Him,
> Jesus Christ who died for me?
>
> Face to face I shall behold Him,
> Far beyond the starry sky;
> Face to face in all His glory,
> I shall see Him by and by!
> (Carrie Ellis Breck)

The promise to
the peacemakers

Blessed are the peacemakers, for they shall be called sons of God.

(Matt. 5:9)

The world needs peacemakers. I think that most of human history has been marked by 'wars and rumors of wars' (Matt. 24:6) and that is certainly true today. However, conflict is not limited to international relations. We find the same thing in families, in the workplace and wherever people come together and seek to do things together. Even the church needs peacemakers! In spite of the words of our Lord Jesus Christ about loving one another (see John 13:34–35), we sometimes forget to do this and instead say harsh things about our brothers and sisters which do not help 'to keep the unity of the Spirit in the bond of peace' (Eph. 4:3).

What causes these conflicts? The Bible says that they come from the sinful desires that exist within each one of us (see James 4:1). We want something and this brings us into conflict with others who want something different. What we want may not be inherently sinful, but it is sinful if we disregard the legitimate desires of others. The first condition for being a peacemaker is to be unselfish. We must 'look out not only for [our] own interests, but also for the interests of others' (Phil. 2:4).

The second condition for being a peacemaker is to address the important issues. Those involved in the conflict will not really be at peace otherwise. It may well flare up again sooner or later. In Old Testament times, there were false prophets who failed to do this. They said, 'Peace, peace!' when there was no peace (Jer. 6:14). They implied that the sinfulness of God's people did not matter; but there could be no true peace with God without repentance.

Galatians 6:1 illustrates this. It sets forth the case of a Christian who has backslidden into sinful ways. What do we do in such a case? Condemn or condone or what? The peacemaker will seek to restore such a person to fellowship with God, but note well the spirit in which this is done: the Bible says 'restore such an one in the spirit of meekness' (KJV). This spirit of meekness is the third condition of being an effective peacemaker. Not 'condemn such an one in the spirit of harshness', nor 'condone such an one in the spirit of indifference', but 'restore such an one in the spirit of meekness'.

The true peacemaker seeks to restore harmony between people in conflict with one another, and also between sinful people and an offended God. In the latter case, the Lord Jesus Christ has already 'made peace through the blood of His cross' (Col. 1:20b). Justice has been satisfied and friendly relations between God and mankind are now possible. All we need to do is to put our trust in the Lord Jesus Christ.

God Himself is the great peacemaker. He was the offended One, but He meekly took the initiative by sending His Son to be our Saviour. The Bible says that 'God was in Christ reconciling the world to Himself' (2 Cor. 5:19). Those who enter into this, by trusting in the Lord Jesus, become peacemakers themselves, copying their Heavenly Father. This is what it means when it says, 'Blessed are the peacemakers, for they shall be called sons of God'—true peacemakers are those who are like their Heavenly Father, and one day they shall be publicly acknowledged before the whole universe (see Rom. 8:19).

The promises to those who are persecuted for righteousness' sake

Blessed are those who are persecuted for righteousness' sake, for theirs is the kingdom of heaven. Blessed are you when they revile and persecute you and say all kinds of evil against you falsely for My sake. Rejoice and be exceedingly glad, for great is your reward in heaven, for so they persecuted the prophets who were before you.

(Matt. 5:10–12)

Most of us do not know much about fierce persecution. In the United Kingdom, Christians are seldom imprisoned or put to death for their faith. However, this Beatitude is not limited to that sort of thing. Our Lord Jesus Christ is talking about the sort of thing that is likely to happen sooner or later to any faithful Christian. People may say bad things ('all kinds of evil') about us—things that are not true ('falsely'). They may insult ('revile') us and exclude us from their company (see Luke 6:22; also John 9:34). Such things are types of persecution, even though they are not as severe as being imprisoned or put to death.

However, the next thing to notice is that the blessing is not 'to those who are persecuted' without qualification, but 'to those who are persecuted for righteousness' sake'. For example, suppose a Christian at work is always telling people about the gospel, but does not do good work in his job. Now, although we should 'always be ready' to tell people about the gospel (1 Peter 3:15), that is not what the Christian in question is being paid for, and if Christians at work do not do a good job then they are, in effect, stealing their wages. If they get into trouble, they are not suffering for righteousness' sake but for stealing, and they cannot claim the blessing of our text.

Righteousness can mean either being right with God or right behaviour. Both can lead to persecution. If we say that we are right with God through the gospel, it implies that others are not, and this will be resented. If we seek to behave rightly, it shows up others who are not doing so and again resentment is likely. The Bible says that 'this is the condemnation, that the light has come into the world and men loved darkness rather than light, because their deeds were evil' (John 3:19). Whether it is the light of the gospel or the light of a holy life, men hate it and would extinguish it if they could.

The first promise to those who are persecuted for righteousness' sake is 'theirs is the kingdom of heaven'. This does not mean that we cannot have assurance of salvation until we have been persecuted, but I think it does mean that persecution for righteousness' sake is the crowning proof (see Phil. 1:27–28) and therefore, surprisingly, a cause for great rejoicing ('rejoice and be exceedingly glad'; e.g. see Acts 5:41).

The second promise is 'great is your reward in heaven'. The Bible is crystal clear that we are saved by grace through faith, 'not of works, lest anyone should boast' (Eph. 2:8–9). However, the Bible also teaches that the Lord Jesus Christ will one day reward what we do for Him after we are saved. This Beatitude is one example of this teaching; see Revelation 22:12 for another.

Our text ends with a reference to 'the prophets'. It reminds us that the people of God are a noble company with a great history:

> They climbed the steep ascent of heaven
> Through peril, toil and pain;
> O God, to us may grace be given
> To follow in their train!
> (Reginald Heber, 'The Son of God Goes Forth to War')

THE PATMOS PROMISES

The promises
attached to the last
book of the Bible

The Revelation of Jesus Christ, which God gave Him to show His servants—things which must shortly take place. And He sent and signified it by His angel to His servant John, who bore witness to the word of God, and to the testimony of Jesus Christ, to all things that he saw. Blessed is he who reads and those who hear the words of this prophecy, and keep those things which are written in it; for the time is near . . .

Behold, I am coming quickly! Blessed is he who keeps the words of the prophecy of this book.

(Rev. 1:1–3; 22:7)

Every book of the Bible is a divine revelation, and this is emphatically true of the last book of the Bible. It is 'the Revelation of Jesus Christ, which God gave Him to show His servants'. It is a divine revelation concerning 'things which must shortly take place'. In other words, it is a prophetic book, and the promises we are considering refer to it as such. From the start of chapter 4 onwards, it is about 'what must take place in the future' (Rev. 4:1, Amplified Bible, Classic Edition). Of course, what was 'future' at the time of writing is not necessarily future now, and Bible teachers disagree about how much has already been fulfilled.

I think some Christians shy away from this wonderful book because there is so much disagreement about its interpretation, and also because it contains so many strange symbols. However, there are explicit promises to those who take to heart its message—the two beatitudes that we are considering—and as Dr Harry Ironside says, God does 'not mean to mock us by promising a blessing on all who keep what they cannot hope to understand!'[1] Christian reader, I urge you to read 'The Revelation of Jesus Christ'. You will not understand all of it, but you *will* understand some of it, by the help of God's Holy Spirit, and it will be a blessing to you.

One reason why it will be a blessing is because the book of Revelation makes us think about the Second Coming of our Lord Jesus Christ, and this can have a very good effect upon us (see 1 John 3:2–3). Another reason why it will be a blessing is that it will lead us to study other parts of the Bible as well. We need to do this in order to understand aright the symbolism of the book of Revelation. Dr Ironside says that 'It may be laid down as a principle of first importance that every symbol used in Revelation is explained or alluded to somewhere else in the Bible.'[2]

For example, the apostle John describes a monster rising up 'out of the sea, having seven heads and ten horns' (Rev. 13:1–2). Obviously, we are not meant to take this literally, but what does it symbolize? It is a lot easier to answer this question if we turn to the book of Daniel, where four monsters are seen coming up from the sea, one of which has ten horns (see Dan. 7:1–7). A careful study of the whole chapter makes it a lot easier to understand the apostle John's monster.

What a wonderful book this book of Revelation is! The Bible would be incomplete without it. It is the capstone of revelation. Just as Genesis tells us how everything began, so Revelation tells us how everything will end. Also, as well as the blessing of the book as a whole, there are five more beatitudes, besides the two we have already considered. These are the subject of the remaining five meditations.

The promise to the
Christian dead

Then I heard a voice from heaven saying to me, 'Write: "Blessed are the dead who die in the Lord from now on."' 'Yes,' says the Spirit, 'that they may rest from their labors, and their works follow them.'

(Rev. 14:13)

Some people would like to focus on the first four words of this beatitude. They would like to say 'Blessed are the dead', regardless of what sort of life they lived while here on earth and regardless of whether or not they were trusting in the Lord Jesus Christ as their Saviour. However, the only ones who are blessed are those 'who die *in the Lord*'—the Christian dead. Otherwise, there is a fearful prospect beyond death, as the preceding verses make plain—see Revelation 14:9–12. Whoever gives their allegiance to the evil that is already at work in this world will share an awful fate in the torment of hell for ever.

In the promise we are considering, the most difficult words to explain are those three little words 'from now on'. The dead who die in the Lord have always been blessed—they go to be with the Lord Jesus Christ in heaven and there is nothing to fear. However, I think the blessing of dying in the Lord is all the greater when viewed against the grim background of fierce antichristian persecution that is portrayed in the previous chapter. Also, there is the stark contrast between the torment of those who give their allegiance to evil and the happiness of those who go to be with their Saviour for ever.

The promise we are considering goes on to speak about

the blessing of rest and the blessing of knowing that the work we have done for the Lord Jesus Christ has been worthwhile. Near the end of his life, the great eighteenth-century evangelist George Whitefield said, 'Lord Jesus, I am weary in Thy work, but not of Thy work', and soon afterwards the Lord gave his willing but weary servant rest from his labours. Christian, now is the time to work for the Lord Jesus Christ with all your heart and soul and strength. A time is coming when you will no longer be able to do so. Work for Him while you can!

We are not saved by works. The Bible says plainly that we are saved by the wonderful grace of God through trusting in the Lord Jesus Christ as our Saviour—it is 'not of works, lest anyone should boast' (see Eph. 2:8–9). However, the Bible assures us that anything we do for the Lord after we become Christians is not in vain. Such works follow us to heaven. They are the 'good works, which God prepared beforehand that we should walk in them' (see Eph. 2:10; 1 Cor. 15:58). God wants us to do them, and one day, in heaven, they will be acknowledged and rewarded.

Christian, do not worry too much about the rewards and honours of this world. What will such things matter when the heavens and the earth are on fire and everything to do with this world is passing away? Work for the Lord and look forward to that day when you will rest from your labours and be with Him for ever.

> When all my labours and trials are o'er,
> And I am safe on that beautiful shore,

Just to be near the dear Lord I adore,
Will through the ages be glory for me.

Oh, that will be glory for me,
Glory for me, glory for me,
When by His grace I shall look on His face,
That will be glory, be glory for me!

When by the gift of His infinite grace
I am accorded in heaven a place,
Just to be there, and to look on His face,
Will through the ages be glory for me.

Friends will be there I have loved long ago;
Joy like a river around me will flow;
Yet just a smile from my Saviour, I know,
Will through the ages be glory for me.
(Chas. H. Gabriel)

The promise to
the well clad

Behold, I am coming as a thief. Blessed is he who watches, and keeps his garments, lest he walk naked and they see his shame.

(Rev. 16:15)

We live in an immodest day and age. People, especially women, appear in public either half naked or else wearing skin-tight clothes that leave little to the imagination. This is neither pleasing to God nor helpful to others. When Adam and Eve sinned in the Garden of Eden, they immediately felt the need to be clothed, and God endorsed this feeling by clothing them with 'long coats of skins' (Gen. 3:21, Amplified Bible, Classic Edition). Likewise, the promise we are considering says that it is a shameful thing to walk naked. However, there is a deeper meaning, just as there was in the Garden of Eden.

The Bible says that 'all our righteousnesses are like filthy rags' (Isa. 64:6). This means that our best efforts to please God, by trying to do what is right, are defiled by sin. It is like coming before a great king wearing filthy rags—we would not be fit for his presence. Likewise, our best efforts to please God do not fit us for His holy presence.

We find the same thing in the book of Zechariah. The prophet had a vision in which Joshua the high priest was standing before the Angel of Jehovah (the pre-incarnate Lord Jesus Christ), 'clothed with filthy garments' (see Zech. 3:1–3). The filthy garments symbolized the fact that Joshua's best efforts to please God were defiled by sin. However, wonderfully, the Angel of Jehovah said that the filthy garments should be taken away, and then said to Joshua, 'See, I have removed your iniquity from you, and I will clothe you with rich robes' (Zech. 3:4).

The rich robes symbolize the righteousness that is imputed to Christians (put to our account). At the Cross, the Lord Jesus Christ satisfied justice by dying in our place, and the Bible says that those who trust in Him are 'justified', or 'declared righteous' (see Rom. 3:24–26). We can come into God's holy presence with confidence because we are clothed with 'the righteousness which is from God by faith' (Phil. 3:9).

The promise we are considering says that the Lord Jesus Christ is 'coming as a thief'. This means that His Second Coming will take many by surprise—they will not be ready for the Day of Judgement. However, if we are trusting in Jesus as our Saviour, then we are well clad and we can look forward to His coming with confidence—so long as we hold fast this confidence 'steadfast to the end' (see Heb. 3:14). This is how we 'keep [our] garments'. Every genuine Christian does this, because 'we are not of those who draw back to perdition, but of those who believe to the saving of the soul' (Heb. 10:39). Continuance proves that we are genuine (e.g. 1 John 2:19).

> Jesus, Thy blood and righteousness
> My beauty are, my glorious dress;
> Midst flaming worlds, in these arrayed,
> With joy shall I lift up my head.

When from the dust of death I rise
To claim my mansion in the skies,
E'en then shall this be all my plea,
Jesus hath lived, hath died, for me!
(Nicolaus Ludwig, Graf von Zinzendorf;
trans. John Wesley)

The promise to the wedding guests

'Let us be glad and rejoice and give Him glory, for the marriage of the Lamb has come, and His wife has made herself ready.' And to her it was granted to be arrayed in fine linen, clean and bright, for the fine linen is the righteous acts of the saints. Then he said to me, 'Write: "Blessed are those who are called to the marriage supper of the Lamb!"' And he said to me, 'These are the true sayings of God.'

(Rev. 19:7–9)

The church is not an organization but a worldwide spiritual entity composed of all true Christians, that is, all who trust in the Lord Jesus Christ as their Saviour, regardless of nationality, status in society or gender—see Galatians 3:28. In the New Testament, it is compared, among other things, to a building, a body and a bride (e.g. Matt. 16:18; 1 Cor. 12:13; Eph. 5:25).

In Bible times, the customary procedure regarding marriage was different from today's. First came the betrothal. This was considered more binding than our 'engagement'. Then, after an interval, the groom went to the home of his bride and took her to his home, where the marriage supper took place. In his commentary on Revelation, *More Than Conquerors*, Dr William Hendriksen says that the festivities used to last for a week or even longer.

The Lord Jesus Christ once told a story about such a marriage. He spoke about 'a certain king who arranged a marriage for his son, and sent out his servants to call those who were invited to the wedding' (see Matt. 22:2–4). However, the invited guests (the Jewish people) 'made light of it' and even badly treated the king's servants (see 22:5–6). The king (God) 'was furious. And he sent out his armies, destroyed those murderers, and burned up their city' (22:7). This was fulfilled in AD 70 when the Roman armies destroyed Jerusalem with much bloodshed.

Since then, the King's servants have been going into all the world, inviting 'all whom they [find], both bad and good', to the marriage supper of the King's Son, the Lord Jesus Christ (see 22:8–10). When we put our trust in Him, our place at that great supper is assured—indeed, the betrothal has already taken place and we have become part of that worldwide spiritual entity which is the Lord's bride (see 2 Cor. 11:2)!

No pre-conversion fitness on our part is required—all are invited, whether good or bad according to human reckoning (we are all bad in God's sight—see Rom. 3:10–12). However, we do need to be 'well clad', as I said in the previous meditation. The man 'who did not have on a wedding garment' was cast 'into outer darkness' (see Matt. 22:11–13). I think we are to assume that all the guests were offered a suitable garment when they came to the marriage supper, but this man refused it; this is why he was 'speechless' when challenged.

I think the wedding garment symbolizes the 'righteousness which is from God by faith', of which I spoke in the previous meditation. It is true that the promise we are considering says that the bride's 'fine linen is the *righteous acts* of the saints' (the Greek simply says 'righteousnesses'). However, the only reason they are clean and bright is because they have been 'washed . . . in the blood of the Lamb' (Rev. 7:14). Apart from that, the Bible says that 'all our righteousnesses [attempts at doing what is right] are like filthy rags' (Isa. 64:6). Our only confidence before God is to trust in the Lord Jesus Christ as our Saviour and to know that His shed blood cleanses us from all sin.

Even the great evangelist Billy Graham found this to be the case. In his very honest autobiography *Just As I Am*, Dr Graham said that when, at the age of eighty-one, he had to undergo major surgery,

> One night a feeling of dread came over me . . . It was almost as if Satan were attacking me (and he may have been), condemning me for my sins, and telling me I was not worthy of a place in heaven. I asked the Lord to help me, and it seemed to me that there was a big screen, and on it appeared a list of all my sins going back to childhood. Then all of a sudden, under them appeared a verse of Scripture: 'The blood of Jesus Christ His Son cleanseth us from all sin' (1 John 1:7, KJV) and I had a great peace that has not left me to this day.[1]

When all who are trusting in Jesus get to heaven for the marriage supper of the Lamb, what a blessed and happy time that will be!

> The bride eyes not her garment,
> But her dear bridegroom's face;

I will not gaze at glory,
But on my King of Grace;
Not at the crown He giveth,
But on His piercèd hand:
The Lamb is all the glory
Of Immanuel's land.
(Samuel Rutherford; A. R. Cousin, 'The Sands of
Time Are Sinking')

The promise that we shall reign with Christ a thousand years

Blessed and holy is he who has part in the first resurrection. Over such the second death has no power, but they shall be priests of God and of Christ, and shall reign with Him a thousand years.

(Rev. 20:6)

The problem with looking at the beatitudes in the book of Revelation is that I have to say something about this one! The trouble is that I have to say something about the Millennium and, *whatever I say*, some of my readers are likely to throw up their hands in holy horror that I should say such a thing! Anyway, I have to say something, so here goes!

The Bible definitely says that a day is coming when Christians will reign with the Lord Jesus Christ (e.g. 2 Tim. 2:11–12a). However, the Bible also says that 'He shall reign forever and ever' (Rev. 11:15; see also Luke 1:33), so what is this about reigning for 'a thousand years' in the promise we are considering?

If I were reading Revelation chapters 19 and 20 for the first time without any preconceived ideas, I think I might conclude that Revelation chapter 19 is a description of the Second Coming and that Revelation chapter 20 is a description of what follows. The devil's agents, 'the beast' and 'the false prophet', are taken and cast into hell at the end of chapter 19 and then the devil himself is laid hold of at the start of chapter 20—it seems to follow on. If it does, then the premillennial interpretation is correct: the Second Coming will usher in a golden age lasting a thousand years, followed by the final judgement of the unsaved dead and the renewal of the whole universe.

However, the problem with the premillennial interpretation is that it is not supported by the rest of the New Testament. There is no passage anywhere else that speaks clearly about such a golden age. Therefore we need to go back to Revelation chapter 20 and ask whether there is another way of explaining it.

The answer is 'yes'. The amillennial interpretation, which I now hold to, points out that the prophetic unfolding of the future in Revelation is not always chronological. For example, as early as the end of chapter 6, we almost reach the Second Coming, but then in subsequent chapters we take a step backwards and get more information about what will happen before that. Here also, in chapter 20, I believe we are taking a step backwards and being given a different viewpoint about what has been going on throughout the present Gospel Age. The 'first resurrection' in the promise we are considering is a spiritual resurrection—I think the reference to 'souls' not 'bodies' in Revelation 20:4 confirms this—and the 'thousand years' simply means a long period of time, namely the present Gospel Age.

The Lord Jesus Christ spoke about a spiritual resurrection when He said that 'the hour is coming, and now is, when the dead will hear the voice of the Son of God; and those who hear will live' (see John 5:24–25). In this present Gospel Age, the spiritually dead hear the voice of the Son of God through the proclamation of the gospel, they put their trust in Him as their Saviour and they receive everlasting spiritual life. The fact that the devil has been laid hold of means that he cannot prevent this—it is 'so that he should deceive the nations no more' (Rev. 20:3)—even though he is still, in other respects, a formidable foe.

When Christians die, they are more alive than ever spiritually. They go to heaven to reign with the Lord Jesus Christ for the rest of the Gospel Age. Then, at the Second Coming, He 'will transform our lowly body that it may be conformed to His glorious body' (Phil. 3:21a), and then we shall reign with Him, not just for a thousand years, but 'forever and ever' (Rev. 22:5)!

The promise to
the washed

Blessed are those who wash their robes, that they may have the right to the tree of life and may go through the gates into the city.

(Rev. 22:14, NIV*)*

The 'city' referred to in the promise we are considering is 'Jerusalem the Golden' which Bernard of Cluny wrote about in a great hymn over eight hundred years ago. It is John Bunyan's Celestial City into which Christian and Hopeful entered with shouting, sound of trumpet and all the bells of the city ringing for joy. It is the wonderful place that God has prepared for those who love Him. The epistle to the Hebrews speaks about the Old Testament heroes of faith and says that '[God] has prepared a city for them' (Heb. 11:16). Also, the words of the Lord Jesus Christ in John 14:1–3 give assurance that this wonderful place is for us as well. At present, it is located 'above' in heaven (Gal. 4:26), but when the created heavens and the earth have been renewed, then the holy city will come down to the new earth, and so will God Himself, to dwell with His people (see Rev. 21:1–3).

The promise we are considering says that some will be allowed to 'go through the gates into [this wonderful] city' and, by implication, others will not. According to the NKJV, those who 'do His commandments' are the ones who will be allowed in, but there is a problem here because it seems to contradict the crystal-clear teaching of the Bible elsewhere that we are 'justified by faith apart from the deeds of the law' (Rom.

3:28). It is true that genuine faith is a living thing that produces good works as its fruit, but I think the simplest way to resolve the problem is to point out that some of the Greek manuscripts from which our English New Testament is translated omit the words 'do His commandments' and say instead 'Blessed are those who *wash their robes*'. Most modern English versions translate it like this, including the NIV which I have used above.

The expression 'wash their robes' links up with Revelation chapter 7 where 'a great multitude which no one could number . . . clothed with white robes' are seen praising God for salvation (Rev. 7:9–10). The whiteness of their robes is attributed not to any goodness of their own, but to the fact that they 'washed their robes and made them white in the blood of the Lamb' (Rev. 7:14; see also John 1:29). We 'wash our robes' when we put our trust in the Lord Jesus Christ as our Saviour. His precious blood cleanses us once and for all from the guilt of sin and we are 'justified', or 'declared righteous'. Then the promise we are considering assures us that we are entitled to 'go through the gates into the city'.

The apostle John tells us in Revelation chapter 21 that the city is glorious to behold, with a great high wall with twelve gates enclosing a vast interior, but what will it be like inside? John tells us that 'the throne of God and of the Lamb' shall be in it, and, because it is a throne of grace, from the throne there will flow 'a pure river of water of life' with 'the tree of life' growing 'on either side of the river' (see Rev. 22:1–2).

The river of the water of *life* and the tree of *life*—this is the everlasting spiritual life of which the gospel speaks (e.g. John 3:16). We cannot see the river at present, but even now it flows to all who trust in the Lord Jesus Christ, and through them to others, bringing satisfaction to their souls (e.g. John 7:37–38). The 'right to the tree of life' was withheld in the Garden of Eden, after Adam sinned (see Gen. 3:22–24). However, by God's grace, this right has been restored, and, in Jerusalem the Golden, we shall enjoy everlasting spiritual life in all its fullness—*if* we are washed in the blood of the Lamb.

Have you been to Jesus for the cleansing power?
Are you washed in the blood of the Lamb?
Are you fully trusting in His grace this hour?
Are you washed in the blood of the Lamb?

Are you washed in the blood,
In the soul-cleansing blood of the Lamb?
Are your garments spotless?
Are they white as snow?
Are you washed in the blood of the Lamb?
(Elisha Albright Hoffman)

Endnotes

Chapter 3 The certainty of the promise

1 H. A. Ironside, *John* (1942; Grand Rapids, MI: Kregel, 2006), p. 150.

Chapter 4 The promise of friendship

1 Albert Midlane, 'The Perfect Righteousness of God'.

Chapter 5 The promise for deep waters

1 Isaac Watts, 'Am I a Soldier of the Cross?'

Chapter 7 The promise that others in our family will be saved

1 Charles H. Spurgeon, *Faith's Checkbook: A 365 Day Devotional* (New Kensington, PA: Whitaker House, 1992), 12 September, 'What of My House?'

Chapter 11 The promise of guidance

1 C. H. Spurgeon, *Treasury of David* (Peabody, MA: Hendrickson, 1990), on Psalm 32:8.

Chapter 12 The promise of provision

1 Geoffrey B. Wilson, *New Testament Commentaries*, Vol. 2 (Edinburgh: Banner of Truth, 2005).

Chapter 15 The promise of an elect company and a warm welcome

1 H. A. Ironside, *Lectures on the Epistle to the Romans* (1928; electronic ed., SolidChristianBooks, 2015), Lecture 6 on Rom. 8.

Chapter 16 The promise of a willing Guest

1 'The Light of the World (Painting)', Wikipedia, https://en.wikipedia.org/wiki/The_Light_of_the_World_(painting).

Chapter 18 The promise to those who mourn

1   M. R. DeHaan, *The Chemistry of the Blood* (Grand Rapids, MI: Zondervan, 1981), p. 139.

Chapter 21 The promise to the merciful

1   Dr Martyn Lloyd-Jones, *Studies in the Sermon on the Mount* (London: Inter-Varsity Press, 1959), p. 99.

Chapter 25 The promises attached to the last book of the Bible

1   H. A. Ironside, *Revelation* (1920; Grand Rapids, MI: Kregel Academic, 2004), p. 11.

2   Harry Ironside, 'The Introduction', *Lectures on the Book of Revelation*, https://bible.prayerrequest.com/4934-harry-ironside-collection-28-files/15/285/.

Chapter 28 The promise to the wedding guests

1   Billy Graham, *Just As I Am* (New York: HarperCollins, 1999), pp. 741–742.